© ALISON PAGE

Amaranth or Pigweed

Amaranthus spp. including
A. retroflexus (amaranth family)

I O A Raw or cooked leaves, stems, flowers. Also seeds. Large herb growing to 3 m. Lance- to oval-shaped leaves up to 15 cm long with visible veins, growing from central stalk. Green to red flowers in dense, furry, upright or drooping clusters.

Habitat: Open, disturbed habitats—gardens, roadsides, fields, empty lots. Taste: Leaves contain oxalic acid, providing a lemony flavour. Eating: Cook leaves and stems like spinach or chard. Toss a few tender greens into salad, or bake leaves into quiche, lasagne or gratin. Seeds can be dried and ground into flour.

© ALLANDA • FOTOLIA.COM

Asparagus

Asparagus officinalis (asparagus family)

P Cooked shoots. Shrub growing 1–1.5 m tall with a slender central stalk (about 1–2 cm in diameter). Foliage appears sparse and feathery with needle-shaped leaves 1–3 cm long. Small, bell-shaped white to yellow flowers singly or in clusters of 2 or 3 form small but conspicuous red berries. ***Do not eat the berries.***

Habitat: Roadsides, railway lines. Harvest: Find plants in summer by foliage and berry appearance, and return in early spring to harvest shoots. Taste: Like store-bought asparagus. Eating: Like store-bought spears: roast, steam, grill, sauté, and add to stirfries, quiches, omelettes, gratins or casseroles.

Chickweed

Stellaria media, S. pallida, S. neglecta (pink family)

U A **Raw or cooked leaves, stems, flowers.** Creeping tender groundcover or small herb to 60 cm. Paired elliptic- to egg-shaped leaves with lines of hairs along leaf stalks and stems. Very small and star-shaped white flowers grow mainly at the end of stems. ***Does not exude milky sap when cut.***

Habitat: Disturbed soil—gardens, lawns, empty lots, fields, parks. Taste: Raw it tastes of corn; cooked resembles very mild spinach. Eating: Add raw to salads, sandwiches, salsa, dips, dressings and smoothies, or cook like spinach and add to stirfries, soups, stews, pasta sauce and casseroles. Avoid during pregnancy.

Chicory

Cichorium intybus (daisy family)

PF P **Raw or cooked leaves, flowers. Also roots.** Tall herb 30–150 cm with branching stem, deep taproot and milky sap. Leaves are alternate, lance-shaped and deeply toothed or lobed; flowers daisy- or dandelion-like but blue, up to 4 cm wide.

Habitat: Roadsides, abandoned fields. Taste: Slightly bitter, like endive or radicchio. Eating: Add young leaves and flowers raw to salads, sandwiches and fresh dips. Leaves can be cooked like spinach in pasta or sauce, and flowers pickled or sugared. Raw roots can be steeped for a coffee-like drink or bittering agent.

Clover

Red: *Trifolium pratense*, White:
T. repens (pea family)

PF **U** **P** **Dried or cooked flowers, cooked young leaves. Also seeds.** Small herb with creeping or erect stems, up to 60 cm, and 3 oval to elliptic leaflets 1–2 cm long. Fragrant white, pink or red clusters of flowers form a dense globe-shape 2 cm wide.

Habitat: Disturbed soil—lawns, fields, parks, roadsides, verges, empty lots. Taste: Flowers are sweet, vanilla-like and slightly nutty. Leaves have a grass-like taste. Eating: Flowers can be tossed raw or roasted into salads, stirfries or soups, or dried for tea. Young leaves can be cooked like spinach with other greens. Seeds are also edible and can be dried and ground into flour.

Curly Dock

Rumex crispus (knotweed family)

U **P** **Cooked young leaves.** Tall herb up to 1 m high forming large circular rosette at base. Large (20–30 cm) elliptical, basal leaves have curly edges, often red along the stem and midrib, ***not hairy***. Clustered on upright stalks, flowers are inconspicuous and small, lacking distinctive petals.

Habitat: Disturbed soil—gardens, parks, roadsides, fields.
Taste: Leaves contain oxalic acid, providing a lemony flavour.
Eating: Cook like spinach in stirfries and sauces, or as a side dish.

Dandelion

Taraxacum officinale (daisy family)

PF **U** **P** **Raw or cooked young leaves, flowers. Also roots**. Small herb growing 5–60 cm with milky sap, taproot and forming a circular rosette at base. Leaves are 5–30 cm, basal, oblong to spoon shaped, and toothed or lobed on edges. Yellow flowers are daisy-like discs on single unbranched stalks.

Habitat: Disturbed soil—gardens, parks, empty lots, verges, road-sides, fields. Taste: Like slightly bitter salad greens. Eating: Young leaves and flowers can be served raw in sandwiches and salads. Cooked leaves can be treated like spinach in sauces, pasta or soups. Roots can be used as a bittering agent, raw or dried.

Daylily

Hemerocallis fulva (asparagus order)

O **P** **Raw or cooked flowers, young leaves, stems. Also tubers.** Small to medium herb 40–150 cm tall. Long (50–90 cm) thin leaves *growing from the base.* Flowers large (5–12 cm), lily-like, *yellow to orange,* and conspicuous, growing *10–20 on a single stalk.*

Habitat: Gardens, landscaping, roadside ditches. Taste: Flowers are crisp and mild. Leaves and stems are similar to mild onions. Eating: Unopened flower heads can be pickled, tossed raw in salads, added to hot and sour soup, or stuffed, battered and pan-fried like squash flowers. Sauté leaves and stems in butter or oil and use like onions.

Fennel
Foeniculum vulgare (carrot family)

I **PF** **O** **P** **Raw or cooked leaves. Also seeds.** Tall herb up to 2.5 m with several hollow stems. Feathery foliage of finely dissected, thread-like leaves only 0.5 mm wide. Large (5–15 cm) umbels, or disc-shaped clusters, of 20–50 tiny yellow flowers.

Habitat: Open sites—gardens, roadsides, verges, fields. Taste: Anise- or black licorice-like greens and seeds. Eating: Toss raw leaves into salads for interesting flavour, or cook into quiche or desserts like panna cotta or clafoutis. Seeds can be ground as a spice.

Fern Fiddleheads, Ostrich and Lady Fern
Matteuccia struthiopteris, Athyrium filix-femina (fern order)

N **O** **P** **Cooked shoots.** Funnel-shaped rosettes 1–2 m tall of unbranched tender fronds growing from central crowns. Ostrich ferns have 5–9 *triangle-shaped* fronds with deeply lobed leaflets from central stalk and no spores (separate brown reproductive fronds). Fiddleheads *6–10 cm wide*, smooth and scale-less with brown, papery flakes and a *deep trough* in upper side of stalk. Lady ferns have 3–7 *diamond-shaped* fronds, deeply lobed leaflets and spores. Fiddleheads *2.5–5 cm wide*, smooth and scale-less with a *shallow trough* in upper side of the stalk.

Habitat: Moist, shady locations—parks, gardens, landscaping. Taste: Mild green with a hint of nuttiness and artichoke. Eating: Like asparagus—steam, sauté, roast, add to quiche or frittata. *Never eat raw.*

Fireweed

Epilobium angustifolium (evening primrose family)

N **PF** **P** **Raw or cooked young leaves and flowers.** Tall herb with unbranched, reddish stems 0.5–3.5 m high. Alternate lance-shaped leaves 5–20 cm long with distinct veins. Flowers 2–4 cm, red to purple with 4 petals, in a cone-shaped cluster of 15–50 at the end of each stem.

Habitat: Moist to dry disturbed soil—ditch sides, roadsides, fields. Taste: Slightly sweet but greens can tend towards bitterness. Eating: Toss raw young leaves and flowers into salads, or cook leaves like spinach in stirfries and soup. Dried leaves and flowers also make good tea, or flowers can be used to make preserves.

Garlic and Field Mustards

Alliaria petiolata and *Brassica campestris, B. rapa, B. vulgaris* (mustard family)

I (garlic mustard) **N** (some mustards) **PF** **P** **Raw or cooked leaves and flowers. Also seeds**. Medium-height herb up to 1 m tall. Leaves alternate, and kidney, arrow or lyre shaped (deeply divided with opposite, paired lobes and larger lobe at end). Flowers grow in clusters and are small, white or yellow, with 4 petals in cross shape. Garlic mustard has a distinct garlic aroma when leaves are crushed.

Habitat: Disturbed soil—roadsides, parks, verges. Taste: Peppery and/or garlicky. Eating: Toss raw leaves and flowers into salads, sandwiches or pesto, or cook in sauces and soup. Seeds can be dried and ground into mustard powder.

Goldenrod

Solidago canadensis or *S. odora*
(daisy family)

N O PF P Raw or cooked
flowers and cooked young leaves.
Also stems. Medium-height herb
growing 40–150 cm with leafy, hairy
stems. Leaves alternate, 2–8 cm long,
lance shaped, often toothed, hairless
or hairy. Flowers are tiny, yellow and in
dense pyramidal clusters at the end of
stems. *Only collect fungus-free leaves.*

Habitat: Disturbed soil—roadsides, parks, forest and wetland
edges. Taste: Faintly sweet, can
be like anise or black licorice
(*S. odora*). Eating: Add raw flowers to salads, desserts, clafoutis,
quiche and preserves. Cook young leaves like spinach in soups, stirfries and stew. Dry leaves and flowers for tea. Stems can be peeled
and pickled.

Kudzu

Pueraria montana (pea family)

I P Shoots, raw or cooked leaves and flowers. Also roots. *Climbing
vine with hairy stems* up to 30 m. Leaves dense, hairy and divided into 3 large
oval leaflets with 2–3 lobes. Flowers 1–3 cm, red to purple in linear clusters like
lupine that point upwards, *with distinct grape-like aroma. Do not eat seeds.*

Habitat: Disturbed soil, agricultural areas. Taste: Grape taste to flowers, mild kale taste to leaves. Eating: Cook shoots like asparagus, toss
young leaves and flowers into salads, bake older leaves like kale chips,
dry leaves and flowers for tea. Roots can be used like potatoes.

Sheep sorrel

Forage for nourishing, flavourful and free food—right in the city! This lightweight, weather-proof, pocket-sized field guide pinpoints edible common weeds—such as curly dock, clover, dandelion, lamb's quarters, plantain, purslane and sheep sorrel—as well as landscaping plants easy to find in urban and suburban settings. Tasty native plants like goldenrod and fireweed are also noted, and readers can eat their way to conservation by learning to recognize edible invasive plants, like garlic mustard and kudzu. Locavores, foodies and the health conscious alike will be able to turn every walk through the neighbourhood into a fun and ecological foraging expedition to make an endless variety of delicious dishes.

Each plant profile is illustrated with a colour photograph and complete with identification, habitat and cooking information—for a total of more than 24 free and fabulous edible plants available in North American cityscapes and suburbs.

MICHELLE CATHERINE NELSON is the author of *The Urban Homesteading Cookbook: Forage, Ferment, Farm and Feast for a Better World* (Douglas & McIntyre, 2015). She has completed a Ph.D. in conservation biology, teaches field ecology and native plant identification, and collects, cooks and preserves all kinds of foraged edibles with her partner in crazy awesomeness, shark biologist Chris Mull.

ISBN 978-1-55017-687-2

HARBOUR PUBLISHING
www.harbourpublishing.com

Text © 2015 Michelle Catherine Nelson
Front and back panel photos by Alison Page
All rights reserved | Printed in South Korea
$8.95